We needed coffee but we'd got ourselves convinced that the later we left it the better it would taste, and, as the country grew flatter and the roads became quiet and dusk began to colour the sky, you could guess from the way we retuned the radio and unfolded the map or commented on the view that the tang of determination had over-taken our thoughts, and when, fidgety and untalkative but almost home, we drew up outside the all-night restaurant, it felt like we might just stay in the car, listening to the engine and the gentle sound of the wind

MATTHEW WELTON was born in Nottingham in 1969 and lives in Manchester. He received the Jerwood-Aldeburgh First Collection Prize for *The Book of Matthew* (Carcanet, 2003), which was a *Guardian* Book of the Year. He was a Hawthornden Fellow in 2004. Matthew collaborates regularly with the composer Larry Goves, with whom he was awarded a Jerwood Opera Writing Fellowship in 2008. He lectures in creative writing at the University of Bolton.

T0096353

Also by Matthew Welton from Carcanet Press

The Book of Matthew

MATTHEW WELTON

We needed coffee but we'd got ourselves
convinced that the later we left it the better
it would taste, and, as the country grew
flatter and the roads became quiet and dusk
began to colour the sky, you could guess
from the way we retuned the radio and
unfolded the map or commented on the
view that the tang of determination had
overtaken our thoughts, and when, fidgety
and untalkative but almost home, we drew
up outside the all-night restaurant, it felt like
we might just stay in the car, listening to the
engine and the gentle sound of the wind

CARCANET

First published in Great Britain in 2009 by
Carcanet Press Limited
Alliance House
Cross Street
Manchester M2 7AQ

A CIP catalogue record for this book is available from the British Library

ISBN 978 1 84777 002 8

The publisher acknowledges financial assistance from Arts Council England

Typeset by XL Publishing Services, Tiverton
Printed and bound in England by SRP Ltd, Exeter

Contents

for Rachel

1
Virtual airport

1

And the moment it takes to blink your eyes and stare, and feel as if you recognise the place you are in, is just long enough for the air to cool off again or the lights to dim, and for the entire feeling of familiarity to drift away to nothing.

The public address plays a mumbling kind of music. The corridor becomes less crowded. A group of girls goes by.

The colour of the light is like new aluminium. A sugary orange-smell carries into the air.

2

The cups of weak coffee and the nylon-colour lighting, the noisy rows we go through and the drifting, hollow music.

3

Like drawings of drawings, or the thoughts of thoughts, the seated figures facing out into the bottle-glass murkiness of the arrivals lounge seem, in a way, to become more absolutely themselves, as if, in taking their place among the magazine kiosks and hot drink machines, they take on a truer understanding of who or what they are, and, in doing so, bring to the buff-colour floor-tiles and plush-effect seating a plainer, steadier, more even perspective.

The light from the windows is like a kind of weariness; the blurry, coloured signboards show nothing that makes much sense.

4

There is a kind of completeness to these families camping out around the restaurant, altogether different from the completeness there is in the colour of the sun, and how it swims over the floor, shifting beyond the shadows of the stools and the chairs.

5

The way the shadow catches the metal of the telephone kiosk gives it the look of something a little out of place. The walkway is empty and the chairs are all empty. The light is like a gesture not everybody is going to understand.

6

There is a sad kind of surprise in the way the steel-colour light takes up the space between the cafeteria and the corridor, giving an even emphasis to the low metal banisters, the pigeon-colour flooring, the wall lamps, the mirroring, the open double doors.

The space itself has the feel of something imagined or something not quite recognised, like getting to your destination and feeling you are still in the place you departed from. Or like returning home and finding no house there, no street, no pavement lined with hedges, your town not even mentioned on the regional travel map.

7

The way the mind sometimes gets these quiet late-winter mornings, the colourless light in the vehicle rentals office and the electric hum from the public address seem to mix in with the usual feeling of uncertainty or distraction, and that other feeling, that there was something you were trying to remember.

8

The sunlight reflecting off the wooden floors; the smell of good coffee; the low curving chairs.

The guy at the window with the girl in the coloured shirt.

The light like something that needn't be explained.

9

The light is like something only dimly understood.

The light is like greaseproof paper.

10

In the time it takes a thought to occur, the feeling that comes with sitting at a table holding a cup of coffee takes on a simple and very positive sort of significance, which will drift away and leave you suddenly sadder, and a little tired.

11

The chairs are the colour of blue chocolate-papers. The departures board is unreadable. The ceilings are low.

The light is like a kind of lengthy explanation – the light is like two thoughts occurring at once.

12

An orange kind of colour like softened wax; a lemon kind of colour; a bright-coloured brown; some green in the blue; some chocolate-colour red; the yellow the colour of a picture-book sun.

13

The fluorescent yellow lighting in the upper-storey corridors is not absolutely like anything you remember.

14

That feeling of sourness you get in the gut, stepping onto a descending escalator, is not unrelated to that trembling sensation – that other feeling you sometimes get – of actually being two places at once.

This is probably something it is better not to talk about.

15

The abrupt bright red of the advertising panels, and the concrete-colour shadows, and the white-painted walls. The blue light reflected in the escalator banister. The almost-green colour of the goods-room window.

16

Wandering out into the softly lit transfers lounge, the feeling you get of something shifting into itself becomes fuller and firmer, simpler and more actual.

There does not have to be any reason for this.

17

The first thing is how much the light from the chandelier brings to mind a pan of bubbling caramel chocolate, and the other's the way the angles of the fluorescent ceiling-tubes are like something from the diagram page of an organic chemistry textbook.

18

Sometimes the light is a soft vanilla-colour; sometimes it is a colour like the yellow of an egg.

19

More than anything, it is for the way the sunlight against the windows gives off a lemony, sugary kind of glow that we imagine we will remember today.

Voices muffle over the tannoy, and an aeroplane idles far off on the concrete.

Somehow we know the moments we live through will carry on happening again and again.

20

The light is a colour like sugar or aspirin; the light is a colour like still lemonade.

21

Waiting out the morning in the roped-off restaurant area, the feeling of looseness and unreality that keeps on bringing us back to ourselves is not unrelated to the certainty we feel as we sit and watch the planes pulling off into the distance, that if we fix our eyes on the names painted along the bodies of the aircraft then we will continue to be able to read those words, never losing focus as the planes become speckles in the vivid deep blue of the sky.

This is nothing much more than a trick to do with distance, like the way our childhoods fasten themselves in the memory always just so far off, so they never seem any more distant or any less real, though further and further away from us they grow.

Warmth comes like a murmur, and the minutes go round. The sunlight at the windows is like honey and butter.

22

In the upstairs lounge the smell of coffee drifts over like the memory of a memory. The ceiling sags like a belly; the light feels incomplete.

The dust-colour shadows spreading over the floor are like hazy little clouds fallen out of the sky.

23

Something about the patterning of the flooring-tiles is like laughing at something you don't quite get. But laughing kind of breathily, and gruffly, and unevenly, and laughing with your voice a little too loud.

24

The middle-morning sunlight, becoming bluish against the windows, creates simple shadows on the sand-colour flooring.

We sit at a table and speak in low voices, and ask for coffee and new ashtrays and paper serviettes.

2

Four-letter words

eins

Push your door shut. Turn down your lamp.
Pour your self some coke. Grab some blue-bean soup.

Some days here it'll feel like it'll grow warm; some days it'll rain.
Take down your book. Play with your biro. Doze till noon.

Then, when some nice dumb idea gets into your mind,
Tune into that folk-rock show.

Don't talk. Don't stir.

Next – *oops!* – some tiny grey bugs will fall onto your desk.
Don't shoo them away.

Don't shoo them away.

zwei

Lose your door keys. Kick over your lamp.
Pour your self some beer. Grab some fish-head stew.

Most days here don't feel that warm – *well well well well* – most days
$\qquad\qquad\qquad\qquad\qquad$ here deep snow will fall.
Chew your lips till they itch. Pour more beer.

Open your note book. Play with your fork. Doze till dusk.

When some zany idea goes – *blam blam* – into your mind,
Play your self some fast – *ding ding* – free – *zing zing* – jazz – *ting ting*
$\qquad\qquad\qquad\qquad\qquad\qquad\qquad\qquad\qquad\qquad$ *ting.*

Stay wary. Don't call home.

Then, when some soft oozy slug gets – *urgh* – onto your desk,
Lock your room. Hide your bike.

Don't undo your coat.

drei

Why'd your back door just slam shut? Why's your room this warm?
D'you want some fizz?

hmmm?

Does your roof leak? How's your wife? Who's that ugly girl?
Why's some body like this need that much cash?

well?

D'you like riot-grrl punk more than lo-fi folk? D'you like blue beat
more than soca?
Soca more than soul? Soul more than glam? Glam more than prog?
Prog more than hard-core sucu suco?

whew...

What have they done with your nice tidy flat?
D'you find you'd have more lice here than itsy pink ants? More bugs
than bees? More grey mice than rats?

funt funk fuse fume fusm fuss futs fuss furk fumn full furd cuck wack
want cunk cuck wack cuck wack cuse wase cume wame cusm wasm
cuss wass cuck wack cuts wats cuss wass curk wark cumn wamn cull
wall curd ward dint arnk jick cont dink arck cose jime dise arme cosm
jiss cose dime arsm coss jick dism arss jits cosm diss arck cots jiss coss
arts coss jirk dits arss cork jimn cots diss arrk comn jill coss dirk armn
coll jird cork dimn arll cord jick comn dill arrd jint coll dird arck cont
jink cord arnt conk jick

slck slck quck shck smck slck shck crck twck frck drck slnt slnt qunt
shnt smnt slnt shnt crnt twnt frnt drnt slnk slnk qunk shnk smnk slnk
shnk crnk twnk frnk drnk slck quck shck smck slck shck crck twck
frck drck slck slck quck shck smck slck shck crck twck frck drck slse
slse quse shse smse slse shse crse twse frse drse slme slme qume shme
smme slme shme crme twme frme drme slsm slsm qusm shsm smsm
slsm shsm crsm twsm frsm drsm slss slss quss shss smss slss shss crss twss
frss drss slck slck quck shck smck slck shck crck twck frck drck slts
slts quts shts smts slts shts crts twts frts drts slss slss quss shss smss slss
shss crss twss frss drss slrk slrk qurk shrk smrk slrk shrk crrk twrk frrk
drrk slmn slmn qumn shmn smmn slmn shmn crmn twmn frmn drmn
slll slll qull shll smll slll shll crll twll frll drll slrd slrd qurd shrd smrd
slrd shrd crrd twrd frrd drrd

fuag fuut cuut fuim cuim waim fuag cuag waag coag fueg cueg waeg
coeg dieg fuit cuit wait wait coit diit arit fuit cuit wait cuit diit fuap
cuap waap coap fuat cuat woat fuig cuig jiag slim piut sleg caim slap
tiag slat toeg slig jeit slat dait slim tuat sleg tuag drat heut drig daim
drat jeag drap toey drit cait dieg piap drag smit sleg sheg shap crag
creg crit crit twim twag tweg twit twil twap frat frim frag freg frit frit
frap frat

fünf

Push your door ajar. Fill your guts with good, weak wine.

Play with your hair. Flip open your head.

coda

Push your, hush
Push your pour your beer your door
More beer more here your more
More push-pull lush-lull hush-mush-mull

Grab your flab, grab your drib-drab crab-slab

blub-blub

Mish-mosh mash; much more such:–
Fish-mash hash-mush dish-rash

Some oozy, lazy loop
Mere dozy, cosy, more hazy
When your door won't open
Must push much more

3
Aimed at nobody

Home economics

for Jo

When it comes to providing an elegant and practical way of making a complaint, a beautiful piece of full-length music lets you join in the fun wherever you are. If you would like a cassette, please call me at home.

Take a look at the table. Pick it up and carry it inside. Forget about your belongings. Your guests have had to go.

Next time you are buying newspapers £118.28 might not be enough. Bedlinen is good for your skin. I am interested in damp clothes.

Measure the circumference of your coffee cups. Position the telephone directly overhead. The moment you touch a vase of flowers you can see up to a mile away.

If dust mites use your central heating to keep warm, or if your orange is stolen or maliciously damaged, or if, when our mother comes to your home, you are not entirely satisfied, you probably should call me.

Snuggle under a cupboard. Change your personal details before your next date.

The habit of warming a lightbulb in your hands seriously inflates your heart.

Got loose and let some

Here's Jesus in the bathroom when the girls have gone.
The bugs crawl up the windows; on the floor there's towels,
and, left out on the table, there's the rolls of film
which Jesus buys for photographing trees he likes.
A talcum smell obliterates the smell of smoke,
and hasn't cleared when, some time later, Jesus grabs
a good weak whisky, puts aside his grammar books
and, pausing at the window on the way downstairs,
rehearses looking louche or gauche, woozy or glum.
You'd never know to look at him how good he feels –
his denims damp and dusty and his hair uncut;
his eyes like dried-up fishes in his dried-up face.

The thing that bothers Jesus as he reaches for
the wall-phone and reiterates in whispers that,
Okay, I'll be right over and that, *Really, no,
that's not a problem*, is how little he's convinced
by what he's saying anymore. Sometimes it's like
the less he speaks, the less he feels the need to speak.
Sometimes a cloud obscures his mind. *Sometimes*, he says,
it's how we love that makes the things we think so sad.
The phone goes. It's for Jesus. Jesus says these words
which inch off down the phonewires like disgruntled bugs.
His voice feels hoarse and hard and loose and, when he's done,
he stays up watching reruns with the sound switched low.

Here's Jesus late last summer when he shows up at
the beach club where the gin's rough and the wine's rough and
the slow things that the band plays fills your head with sludge.
If Jesus gets the notion to sit in and jam,
you probably better split or you'll be here all night
because when Jesus blows harmonica it's like
his mind got loose and let some drumming, drawling thought
come rumbling from the reaches of the universe
so almost abruptly that it gets in the way
of where he's at and leaves him tired and tense and bored.
Most days he stays home, slumped on the couch, slugging on
a rum-and-lemon, wondering what he's in for next.

Clued in

Nervy old worms
located everybody's sneakers, so everybody reacted
by rushing into the infirmary. Somebody humble
here engineers rainclouds. Our
hypnotherapist offers lithium doses. Say
that he's edgy;
purchase a shorter skirt.

But until tonight
let anybody suggest the
bastard's losing out. We
wanted another shortbread
biscuit; everybody loves a tickle – even divorcees.
Industrialisation never
happened. It's surprisingly
pleasant remaining indoors, discussing electrocution.

Paul Simon variations

I'm laying out my winter clothes.
      I'm laying out my winter girl.
            I'm laying up my winter girl.
I'm fucking up my winter girl.
      I'm fucking up my Spanish girl.
            I'm fucking up your Spanish girl.
Who's fucking up your Spanish girl?

If I had a yammer

Our neighbours next door
They gave us this saw

That's as long as a song
And as sharp as a claw

Underneath it's got teeth
Which you should not ignore

And it cuts through the ceiling
And cuts up the floor

But it's never much good in a drench
So perhaps what we need is a wrench

*

Our friends who speak French
They gave us this wrench

And we use it to grip
And to grasp and to clench

It's as tight as a bite
And as strong as a stench

And it's firm like a worm
With its bum on a bench

But it's never much good in a chill
So perhaps what we need is a drill

*

A boy who felt ill
He gave us this drill

And we find that we wind it
And grind it until

There are holes in our souls
And a hole in the hill

That a sackful of sand
and cement couldn't fill

But it's never much good against fires
So perhaps what we need is some pliers

★

A bunch of old liars
They gave us these pliers

Which have wonderful ways
Of connecting with wires

And they twist like a wrist
Or a chorus of choirs

'Til they get us so giddy
We're squealing like tyres

But they're never much good when it hails
So perhaps what we need is some nails

★

A girl from South Wales
She gave us these nails

And we keep them in cupboards
And weigh them with scales

And we put them in plant-pots
And pitchers and pails

'Til it makes us so mad
We go right off the rails

But they're never much good in a thaw
So perhaps what we need after all is a saw

Woven poems

summer pumpkin

pwmpen mai

★

honeyfish

sgodyn mêl

★

mooses and gooses

ysgwyddau a gwyddau

Poppy

Scout puts a record on. In the kitchen sits Tujiko. Naomi and Damon eat too much rice. I came back from São Paulo expecting twins.

Joanna and Rachid have a feel for the seasons and an amateur interest in entomology. I cycled slowly into the small green field. Somewhere on the tape there's someone singing hymns.

After the sun sets, the sound of a piano is like a gradual fluctuation in the colour of the clouds. The birds were reappearing; the wind is on its way.

Bailey is thought to have abandoned his wife in a house in Manhattan built from small wooden blocks. The store proprietor drove through London. Mika and Philippe are righteous people.

Ursula started to bore me. Thurston started to bore me. Sunlight becomes twilight; flowers bloom and it rains. McGregor restrains his impressive voice.

I never understood my conversation with Didi. I expect Jakob to separate from Yoshimi, his wife. My older brother stood away from my friends. I'm sitting on a sofa with maracas in my hands.

I must say that at first it was difficult work

A malaise that affects the demented at first
A masseuse with a thirst for delicious liqueurs
A monsieur who's inferring that discipline hurts
A moose in wet weather is disturbed as he walks
A mosquito, a butterfly, a tickler, a worm
A mouse with white fur was sick in the water

A mushroom that occurs in deciduous woods
An assailant who's certain of judicial mercy
And I'm saving the termites for further research
And most of the term he was dead to the world
And my cousin whose burps are not typical burps
And myxomatosis has stiffened its fur

Aramaic inverts the intransitive verbs
As potatoes emerge from the depths of the earth
I'm arranging excursions to disparate worlds
I'm assured there's a version that's technically worse
I'm a surgeon who's working with domicile birds
I'm elated to learn I'm in step with the herd

I'm okay but I've heard that there's dozens who weren't
I'm the same as my father who entered the church
I'm untrained but alert to this miniscule surge
It's my serious aversion to the demands of women
She masqueraded as a desperate girl
The inmates of the infirmary weep deeply for her

The Mercedes is hers but she drives in reverse
The messiah was the worst for discussing the waitresses
The mezuzahs affixed to the dayanim's walls
The mistake of resuming indifferent rehearsals
The mist and the frost – devastating white
The muscular flirt with the definite curves

The music in the verse is a discordant waltz
The music, rehearsed with different words
The music station in Amherst was affected the worst
The mystery woman is dispatched to the wardrobe
Unashamed and impertinent, distant, unnerved
Unassuming and furtive and stiff and absurd

Measure

for Keith

You weigh, cremated, what you weighed at birth.

4

South Korea and Japan 2002

Group stage

31 May   Seoul Stadium, South Korea
There's this senile feeling of tiredness to the colours in the sky; and
this other feeling in the stomach, like something put up for franchise.

01 June   Ibaraki Kashima Stadium, Japan
The views across the river from the rooms upstairs are like the pages
of a book that no one would republish; the thoughts we recall from
our drive to the store appear to us now like an unpromising kind of
camouflage.

01 June   Ulsan Munsu Stadium, South Korea
And after the friends who had brought us here drove out again into
the dawn, we idled away our morning in that cheaply furnished den
of iniquity.

01 June   Sapporo Dome, Japan
The smell out on the landing is like fresh grass and germicide; in the
kitchen the smell is like sauerkraut and sawdust.

02 June   Ibaraki Kashima Stadium, Japan
There's a sort of argy-bargy in the rainclouds and the wind as you
stand there in the carpark like a niggard in new shoes.

02 June   Busan Asiad Main Stadium, South Korea
From the window of our apartment in the southeast reach of the city,
we sometimes get to see the parakeets in the trees at the zoological
gardens.

02 June   Saitama Stadium, Japan
The colour of the light engorging into the late-summer sky sweeps
away the uncertainties we'd been feeling up until now.

02 June   Gwangju Stadium, South Korea
These feelings of uncertainty seemed to span the days we spent here;
there is something almost slovenly about the shadows spread out in
the grass.

03 June   Niigata Stadium Big Swan, Japan
Out on the mezzanine at the Museum of Spontaneous Art, the thoughts and ideas we crochet together put us on edge for the rest of the night.

03 June   Ulsan Munsu Stadium, South Korea
With the breezes from the south breaking like brazil nuts, we turkey around in the afternoon sun, getting shriller and louder and maybe a little dizzy.

03 June   Sapporo Dome, Japan
There's the itch we feel to be away from here tonight; and then the stubbornness we feel feels ecumenical and unsure.

04 June   Gwangju Stadium, South Korea
Drinking milky coffee from blue china cups, the wind across the garden feels cost-effective and contrived.

04 June   Saitama Stadium, Japan
You come in undressed with that smile on your face, your belly button hidden by the way that you stand, and we just can't help but jape around, talking too hurriedly, and singing too loud.

04 June   Busan Asiad Main Stadium, South Korea
The wind comes in like some skinny little southpaw – the feelings we have over leaving seem certain and vivid and polarised.

05 June   Kobe Wing Stadium, Japan
We tunnel away at the same few ideas, and the insides of our minds seem to soften up like rust.

05 June   Suwon Stadium, South Korea
Our memories of the days we spent in this house take on a worrying new usability – the view of the trees from this side of the house would be something impossible to pose.

05 June   Ibaraki Kashima Stadium, Japan
The view of the garden from the room downstairs is like a page from
a book no one would republish; the smell on the landing is like
germicide or stale water.

06 June   Daegu Stadium, South Korea
As we idled out our afternoon in that softly lit den of iniquity, there
was this senile feeling of certainty to the sunlight fading out in the
sky.

06 June   Saitama Stadium, Japan
The journey we remember we made to the stadium comes back to
us now as a sad kind of camouflage; the smell in our room is like
sauerkraut and limes.

06 June   Busan Asiad Main Stadium, South Korea
After the friends who had brought us here had set off into the dawn,
there was that feeling again in the stomach – like something being
put up for franchise.

07 June   Kobe Wing Stadium, Japan
You stand here in the hallway like a niggard with new shoes, and in
sweeps the affection we'd been missing until now.

07 June   Jeonju Stadium, South Korea
A feeling of determination seems to span the summers we spend here;
we look for the redwinged parakeet in the tree at the zoological park.

07 June   Sapporo Dome, Japan
There's a kind of argy-argy in the rainclouds and the sun, and the
colour of the light in the low summer sky engorges through the trees
and flowers.

08 June   Daegu Stadium, South Korea
From the living room of our walk-up in the southeast section of the
city, we notice something almost slovenly in the flowers that grow
in the grass.

08 June   Ibaraki Kashima Stadium, Japan
There's the itch we feel just to get in the car and drive 'til there's light in the sky; the worries and misgivings we crochet together give us a buzz for the rest of the night.

08 June   Jeju Stadium, South Korea
Drinking sugary coffee from shallow china cups – the rainclouds from the south breaking like brazil nuts.

09 June   Miyagi Stadium, Japan
Down on the mezzanine at the Museum of Mathematical Art, the anxiety we feel seems ecumenical and aloof.

09 June   Incheon Munhak Stadium, South Korea
The wind this summer feels cost-effective or compulsive, and we turkey about, feeling giggly and sad.

09 June   International Stadium Yokohama, Japan
The insides of our minds seem to soften like loose rust, and we just can't help but jape around, shouting our names out and scratching at our hands.

10 June   Daegu Stadium, South Korea
The breeze comes in like an underweight southpaw, and your memories of the summer have an unsettling usability.

10 June   Oita Stadium Big Eye, Japan
You walk in undressed with a frown on your face, your belly button hidden by the way you hold your arms, and we tunnel away at the same old ideas, a raspberry-colour sunlight washing against the walls.

10 June   Jeonju Stadium, South Korea
There is still something polarised about the feelings we're left with; the view of the trees this time of night is something you couldn't either pose or forget.

11 June   Incheon Munhak Stadium, South Korea
As we idle out the evening in this overcrowded den of iniquity, there's this feeling we get in the belly like something offered for franchise.

11 June   Suwon Stadium, South Korea
There's a senile sense of distraction to the watery, colourless sky as the friends we invited arrive around dawn.

11 June   Shizuoka Stadium Ecopa, Japan
The smell on the stairs is like undiluted germicide; the journeys we took come back to us now as a suspicious sort of camouflage.

11 June   International Stadium Yokohama, Japan
The smell on the steps is like sauerkraut and vodka; the memories we have of that small, clean room are like pictures no one would republish.

12 June   Miyagi Stadium, Japan
After the argy-bargy with the rain and the wind and the sun, you sweep away the distractedness I think I'd begun to feel.

12 June   Nagai Stadium, Japan
The yellow-colour light in the early-morning sky engorges into the trees by the lake as you come across the carpark like a niggard in new shoes, smiling and talking and flagging your hands.

12 June   Daejeon Stadium, South Korea
This feeling of recrimination seems to span the months we spend here in these generous and tidy apartments in the southeast portion of the city.

12 June   Jeju Stadium, South Korea
Trying to describe the parakeets in the trees at the zoological park, we begin to see something slovenly and sad in the leaves drying out in the grass.

13 June   Suwon Stadium, South Korea
The winds from the south feel cost-effective and unquiet and break like brazil nuts in the late afternoon.

13 June   Seoul Stadium, South Korea
Drinking hot coffee from small china cups, we turkey around in the afternoon heat, getting steadier and slower and more intense.

13 June   Oita Stadium Big Eye Japan
Over on the mezzanine at the Museum of Liquid Art, the itch we feel to be back by tonight drifts slowly away into nothing.

13 June   International Stadium Yokohama, Japan
This fragility we feel seems ecumenical and unfair; the needs and wants we crochet together leave us alone for the rest of the night.

14 June   Nagai Stadium, Japan
We tunnel away with the one idea as the skin on our arms gets damp and loose, and we just can't help but jape around, finishing the wine and talking too slowly.

14 June   Shizuoka Stadium Ecopa, Japan
You came in undressed with a grin on your face, your belly button hidden by the way you walk; the insides of my mind collapse like loose rust.

14 June   Incheon Munhak Stadium, South Korea
And when the wind cuts in like some ribby little southpaw, the view from this hill is like nothing you could pose.

14 June   Daejeon Stadium, South Korea
As our feelings about our feelings become polarised and more rational, our feelings about our memories have a bizarre new usability, a particular sort of clarity even we don't understand.

Second round

15 June   Jeju Stadium, South Korea
The smell out in the street is like double-strength germicide; we count the redwinged parakeets in the grounds at the zoological park.

15 June   Niigata Stadium, Japan
As we idle out an afternoon in this glass-walled den of iniquity, the orange-colour light in the early-autumn sky engorges into the road-side trees.

16 June   Oita Stadium Big Eye, Japan
There's this senile feeling of aimlessness to the clouds set out in the sky, which sweeps away the caution we'd been hanging on to until now.

16 June   Suwon Stadium, South Korea
A feeling of aloneness seems to span the mornings we spend here; the view across the garden from the kitchen upstairs is like a book which won't get republished.

17 June   Jeonju Stadium, South Korea
Down on the mezzanine at the Museum of Ontological Art, the usability we find our memories acquire causes us to laugh or scratch at our wrists.

17 June   Kobe Wing Stadium, Japan
With the sound of the wind breaking like brazil nuts, you walk out undressed with a squint on your face, your belly button hidden by the way you move.

18 June   Miyagi Stadium, Japan
We just can't help but turkey around, screaming like monkeys 'til late in the night; we feel this need to jape around, saying things loudly we don't understand.

18 June   Daejeon Stadium, South Korea
As the wind rumbles in like an overweight southpaw, the itch we feel to pack the car and go is vivider and realer and harder to ignore.

Quarter-finals

21 June   Shizuoka Stadium, Japan
The sounds along the freeway breaking like brazil nuts – the stone-colour light engorging the unploughed fields.

21 June   Ulsan Stadium, South Korea
The melody we remembered so carefully all winter has for us now little use or usability – the smells on our hands are of germicide and metal.

22 June   Gwangju Stadium, South Korea
The summer hurries on like some unfancied southpaw, and a feeling of aloneness seems to span the months we have left.

22 June   Nagai Stadium, Japan
There's that senile feeling of wantlessness about the night we left by taxi when we just couldn't help but turkey around, clenching our fingers like bunches of shrimps.

Semi-finals

25 June   Seoul Stadium, South Korea
The smell on our clothes is like lemon-scented germicide, the wind
comes on slowly like a southpaw out of shape.

26 June   Saitama Stadium, Japan
Those evenings with the music breaking like brazil nuts, we'd turkey
around at the back of the house, talking with our voices turned low.

Third-place play-off

The wind holds off like an overthoughtful southpaw, and we just can't help but turkey around, removing our shoes and trying to look relaxed.

World Cup Final

30 June   Yokohama International Stadium, Japan
The silence in the kitchen breaking like brazil nuts – the smell of
damp or germicide unwashable from our winter clothes.

5

Six poems by themselves

for Nik

The poem in itself

_____

_____

_____

_____

_____

_____

_____

_____

_____

_____

_____

_____

The poem as itself

_____
_____
_____
_____
_____
_____

_____
_____
_____
_____
_____
_____

The poem to itself

_____

_____

_____

_____

_____

_____

_____

_____

_____

_____

_____

_____

The poem so itself

_____
_____
_____

_____
_____
_____

_____
_____
_____

_____
_____
_____

The poem or itself

_____
_____

_____
_____

_____
_____

_____
_____

_____
_____

_____
_____

The poem of itself

_____

_____

_____

_____

_____

_____

_____

_____

_____

_____

_____

6
Dr Suss

1

In her trainers and jeans she looks like a narrow-faced Alastair Burnet. In her trainers and jeans she looks like a sad-faced Albert Einstein. In her trainers and jeans she looks like a wary-faced Albertus Magnus. In her trainers and jeans she looks like a sour-faced Angelica Huston. In her trainers and jeans she looks like a sallow-faced Anna Ford. In her trainers and jeans she looks like a thin-faced Aristotle. In her trainers and jeans she looks like a blue-faced Arthur Schopenhauer. In her trainers and jeans she looks like a glum-faced Audrey Hepburn. In her trainers and jeans she looks like an elegant-faced Barnes Wallis. In her trainers and jeans she looks like a white-faced Bartolomeu Dias. In her trainers and jeans she looks like a mustard-faced Benny Hill. In her trainers and jeans she looks like a gloomy-faced Bernard Manning. In her trainers and jeans she looks like a daisy-faced Bertrand Russell. In her trainers and jeans she looks like a plump-faced Bette Davis. In her trainers and jeans she looks like a meaty-faced Blériot. In her trainers and jeans she looks like a cotton-faced Bo Derek. In her trainers and jeans she looks like an oily-faced Bob Hope. In her trainers and jeans she looks like a fish-faced Bob Monkhouse. In her trainers and jeans she looks like a long-faced Bobby Charlton.

2

Late in the evening over beer and cold hot-dogs, she hums me the folksongs she learned from Bobby Moore. Late in the evening over beer and cold hot-dogs, she hums me the melodies she learned from Boethius. Late in the evening over beer and cold hot-dogs, she hums me the refrains she learned from Bononcini. Late in the evening over beer and cold hot-dogs, she hums me the riffs she learned from Boris III. Late in the evening over beer and cold hot-dogs, she hums me the skipping-rhymes she learned from Boris Yeltsin. Late in the evening over beer and cold hot-dogs, she hums me the variations she learned from Bronzino. Late in the evening over beer and cold hot-dogs, she hums me the show tunes she learned from Bruce Forsyth. Late in the evening over beer and cold hot-dogs, she hums me the calypsos she learned from Burt Kwouk. Late in the evening over beer and cold hot-dogs, she hums me the marches she learned from Burt Lancaster. Late in the evening over beer and cold hot-dogs, she hums me the harmonies she learned from Buster Keaton. Late in the evening over beer and cold hot-dogs, she hums me the cello suites she learned from Byrd. Late in the evening over beer and cold hot-dogs, she hums me the quartets she learned from Cabral. Late in the evening over beer and cold hot-dogs, she hums me the arias she learned from Calvin. Late in the evening over beer and cold hot-dogs, she hums me the hymns she learned from Captain Cook. Late in the evening over beer and cold hot-dogs, she hums me the jingles she learned from Cary Grant. Late in the evening over beer and cold hot-dogs, she hums me the duets she learned from Charles Darwin. Late in the evening over beer and cold hot-dogs, she hums me the choruses she learned from Chen Yizi. Late in the evening over beer and cold hot-dogs, she hums me the solos she learned from Cher. Late in the evening over beer and cold hot-dogs, she hums me the right-hands she learned from Chiang Kai-shek. Late in the evening over beer and cold hot-dogs, she hums me the ballads she learned from Chico. Late in the evening over beer and cold hot-dogs, she hums me the concertos she learned from Chou En-lai. Late in the evening over beer and cold hot-dogs, she hums me the studies she learned from Chris Waddle. Late in the evening over beer and cold hot-dogs, she hums me the waltzes she learned from Chu Teh. Late in the evening over beer and cold hot-dogs, she hums me the verses she learned from Cicero. Late in the evening over beer and cold hot-dogs, she hums me the preludes she learned from Colin Powell. Late in the evening over beer and cold hot-dogs, she hums me the cantos she learned from Columbus. Late in the evening over beer and cold hot-dogs, she hums me the chords she learned from Corelli. Late in the evening over beer and cold hot-dogs, she hums me the introductions she learned from Cosimo Tura. Late in the evening over beer and cold hot-dogs, she hums me the crescendos she learned from David Niven. Late in the evening over beer and cold hot-dogs, she hums me the codas she learned from Deng Xiaoping. Late in the evening over beer and cold hot-dogs, she hums me the descants she learned from Des Walker. Late in the evening over beer and cold hot-dogs, she hums me the hooks she learned from Dick Cheney. Late in the evening over beer and cold hot-dogs, she hums me the psalms she learned from Diego Maradona. Late in the evening over beer and cold hot-dogs, she hums me the symphonies she learned from Dosso Dossi. Late in the evening over beer and cold hot-dogs, she hums me the notes she learned from Ed Murrow. Late in the evening over beer and cold hot-dogs, she hums me the blues she learned from Edmund Hillary. Late in the evening over beer and cold hot-dogs, she hums me the rumbas she learned from Epicurus. Late in the evening over beer and cold hot-dogs, she hums me the themes she learned from Eric Morecambe and Ernie Wise. Late in the evening over beer and cold hot-dogs, she hums me the polkas she learned from Eric Sykes. Late in the evening over beer and cold hot-dogs, she hums me the counterpoints she learned from Eric the Red. Late in the evening over beer and cold hot-dogs, she hums me the rhythms she learned from Ernest Shackleton. Late in the evening over beer and cold hot-dogs, she hums me the rounds she learned from Fawn Hall. Late in the evening over beer and cold hot-dogs, she hums me the drones she learned from Ferdinand Magellan.

3

Getting into the car on the south side of Main Street, 'It's just a lot of cold treacle,' was all Filippino Lippi would say. Getting into the car on the south side of Main Street, 'It's just a lot of lumpy treacle,' was all Flanagan and Allen would say. Getting into the car on the south side of Main Street, 'It's just a lot of bad treacle,' was all Fontana would say. Getting into the car on the south side of Main Street, 'It's just a lot of warm treacle,' was all Fra Angelico would say. Getting into the car on the south side of Main Street, 'It's just a lot of smooth treacle,' was all Fra Filippo Lippi would say. Getting into the car on the south side of Main Street, 'It's just a lot of personal treacle,' was all Francis Chichester would say. Getting into the car on the south side of Main Street, 'It's just a lot of unfortunate treacle,' was all Francis Drake would say. Getting into the car on the south side of Main Street, 'It's just a lot of nasty treacle,' was all Francisco Pizarro would say. Getting into the car on the south side of Main Street, 'It's just a lot of expensive treacle,' was all Frank Whittle would say. Getting into the car on the south side of Main Street, 'It's just a lot of musical treacle,' was all G.F. Handel would say. Getting into the car on the south side of Main Street, 'It's just a lot of monstrous treacle,' was all Galileo would say. Getting into the car on the south side of Main Street, 'It's just a lot of fancy treacle,' was all Gao Xin would say. Getting into the car on the south side of Main Street, 'It's just a lot of technical treacle,' was all Gary Lineker would say. Getting into the car on the south side of Main Street, 'It's just a lot of modern treacle,' was all Geoff Hurst would say. Getting into the car on the south side of Main Street, 'It's just a lot of tiresome treacle,' was all Georg Hegel would say. Getting into the car on the south side of Main Street, 'It's just a lot of beautiful treacle,' was all George Best would say. Getting into the car on the south side of Main Street, 'It's just a lot of religious treacle,' was all George Burns would say. Getting into the car on the south side of Main Street, 'It's just a lot of self-righteous treacle,' was all George Bush would say. Getting into the car on the south side of Main Street, 'It's just a lot of tasty treacle,' was all George Stephenson would say. Getting into the car on the south side of Main Street, 'It's just a lot of greasy treacle,' was all Gerard Hoffnung would say. Getting into the car on the south side of Main Street, 'It's just a lot of modern treacle,' was all Gian Paolo

Cima would say. Getting into the car on the south side of Main Street, 'It's just a lot of awkward treacle,' was all Gina Lollobrigida would say. Getting into the car on the south side of Main Street, 'It's just a lot of thick treacle,' was all Googie Withers would say. Getting into the car on the south side of Main Street, 'It's just a lot of sweet treacle,' was all Gordon Banks would say. Getting into the car on the south side of Main Street, 'It's just a lot of sophisticated treacle,' was all Gottlieb Daimler would say. Getting into the car on the south side of Main Street, 'It's just a lot of raucous treacle,' was all Grace Kelly would say.

A slow summer breeze through the first-storey window, Groucho smoking at the bathroom sink. A delicate summer breeze through the first-storey window, Guglielmo Marconi smoking at the bathroom sink. A sudden summer breeze through the first-storey window, Gummo smoking at the bathroom sink. A fresh summer breeze through the first-storey window, Harpo smoking at the bathroom sink. A hard summer breeze through the first-storey window, Helmut Kohl smoking at the bathroom sink. A cool summer breeze through the first-storey window, Henri I smoking at the bathroom sink. An imaginary summer breeze through the first-storey window, Henri II smoking at the bathroom sink. A regrettable summer breeze through the first-storey window, Henri III smoking at the bathroom sink. An unpleasant summer breeze through the first-storey window, Henri IV smoking at the bathroom sink. A firm summer breeze through the first-storey window, Henry Fonda smoking at the bathroom sink. A dense summer breeze through the first-storey window, Henry Ford smoking at the bathroom sink. A tight summer breeze through the first-storey window, Henry Purcell smoking at the bathroom sink. An occasional summer breeze through the first-storey window, Henry the Navigator smoking at the bathroom sink. An unforecast summer breeze through the first-storey window, Hernando Cortes smoking at the bathroom sink. A Californian summer breeze through the first-storey window, Hsueh-liang smoking at the bathroom sink. A comfortable summer breeze through the first-storey window, Hu Guofeng smoking at the bathroom sink. A forceful summer breeze through the first-storey window, Hu Yaobang smoking at the bathroom sink. An endless summer breeze through the first-storey window, Humphrey Bogart smoking at the bathroom sink. A noticeable summer breeze through the first-storey window, Immanuel Kant smoking at the bathroom sink. A foggy summer breeze through the first-storey window, Isaac Newton smoking at the bathroom sink. A light summer breeze through the first-storey window, Isambard Kingdom Brunel smoking at the bathroom sink. A northerly summer breeze through the first-storey window, J.P. Sweelinck smoking at the bathroom sink. A mournful summer breeze through the first-storey window, J.S. Bach smoking at the bathroom sink. A loud summer breeze through the first-storey window, J.S. del Cano smoking at the bathroom sink. A reticent summer breeze through the first-storey window, Jack Benny smoking at the bathroom sink. A low summer breeze through the first-storey window, Jack Lemmon smoking at the bathroom sink. A lemony summer breeze through the first-storey window, Jacques Tati smoking at the bathroom sink. A slack summer breeze through the first-storey window, Jacques-Yves Cousteau smoking at the bathroom sink. A lilting summer breeze through the first-storey window, James Baker smoking at the bathroom sink.

'And I *was* feeling a *little* worried before you even mentioned James Watt.'

'And I *was* feeling a *little* goofy before you even mentioned Jamie Lee Curtis.'

'And I *was* feeling a *little* fearful before you even mentioned Jane Fonda.'

'And I *was* feeling a *little* troubled before you even mentioned Janet Leigh.'

'And I *was* feeling a *little* flummoxed before you even mentioned Jean Harlow.'

'And I *was* feeling a *little* lost before you even mentioned Jean-Paul Sartre.'

'And I *was* feeling a *little* underdressed before you even mentioned Jean Simmons.'

'And I *was* feeling a *little* inadequate before you even mentioned Joan Chen.'

6

As slow as winter fog, we set out for our appointment with John Barnes. As slow as winter fog, we missed our appointment with John Cabot. As slow as winter fog, we returned to our appointment with John Huston. As slow as winter fog, we apologised for our appointment with John Locke. As slow as winter fog, we rescheduled our appointment with John Logie Baird. As slow as winter fog, we remembered our appointment with John Sham. As slow as winter fog, we explained our appointment with John Simpson. As slow as winter fog, we drove back from our appointment with John Wayne. As slow as winter fog, we did something about our appointment with Jupiter.

Karl Marx, sober and alone, standing at the window with the phone in his hand. Kate Adie, tearful and alone, standing at the window with the phone in her hand. Katherine Hepburn, indignant and alone, standing at the window with the phone in her hand. Ken Dodd, relaxed and alone, standing at the window with the phone in his hand. Kenneth Kendall, alert and alone, standing at the window with the phone in his hand. Kierkegaard, resigned and alone, standing at the window with the phone in his hand. King Faud, suspicious and alone, standing at the window with the phone in his hand. Kirk Douglas, panicky and alone, standing at the window with the phone in his hand. Lauren Bacall, obsessed and alone, standing at the window with the phone in her hand. Laurence Olivier, unwell and alone, standing at the window with the phone in his hand. Leonard Rossiter, unprepared and alone, standing at the window with the phone in his hand. Leonardo da Vinci, depressed and alone, standing at the window with the phone in his hand. Les Dawson, thoughtful and alone, standing at the window with the phone in his hand. Li Xiannian, breathless and alone, standing at the window with the phone in his hand.

Sitting outside the delicatessen, Lin Piao with the sun warming his face. Sitting outside the delicatessen, Liu Shao Chi with the sun softening his face. Sitting outside the delicatessen, Louis I with the sun roughening his face. Sitting outside the delicatessen, Louis II with the sun burning his face. Sitting outside the delicatessen, Louis III with the sun opening his face. Sitting outside the delicatessen, Louis IV with the sun leavening his face. Sitting outside the delicatessen, Louis IX with the sun colouring his face. Sitting outside the delicatessen, Louis V with the sun reaching his face. Sitting outside the delicatessen, Louis VI with the sun brightening his face. Sitting outside the delicatessen, Louis VII with the sun leaving his face. Sitting outside the delicatessen, Louis VIII with the sun weakening his face. Sitting outside the delicatessen, Louis X with the sun waking his face. Sitting outside the delicatessen, Louis XI with the sun texturing his face. Sitting outside the delicatessen, Louis XII with the sun lightening his face. Sitting outside the delicatessen, Louis XIII with the sun saddening his face. Sitting outside the delicatessen, Louis XVIII with the sun marbling his face. Sitting outside the delicatessen, Louis Pasteur with the sun swarming his face. Sitting outside the delicatessen, Mao Tse-tung with the sun swamping his face. Sitting outside the delicatessen, Marat with the sun contorting his face. Sitting outside the delicatessen, Marco Polo with the sun reddening his face. Sitting outside the delicatessen, Marie Curie with the sun hurting her face.

We imagine Marin Marais, the winter-morning sunlight in the branches of the trees. We imagine Mars, the late-morning sunlight in the branches of the trees. We imagine Martin Heidegger, the full morning sunlight in the branches of the trees. We imagine Max Wall, the gentle morning sunlight in the branches of the trees. We imagine Mel Brooks, the yellow morning sunlight in the branches of the trees. We imagine Mercury, the dull morning sunlight in the branches of the trees. We imagine Michael Caine, the artificial morning sunlight in the branches of the trees. We imagine Michael Faraday, the thursday-morning sunlight in the branches of the trees. We imagine Michelangelo, the relentless morning sunlight in the branches of the trees. We imagine Mme du Barry, the restless morning sunlight in the branches of the trees. We imagine Monteverdi, the colourless morning sunlight in the branches of the trees. We imagine Napoleon, the uncertain morning sunlight in the branches of the trees. We imagine Naudot, the growing morning sunlight in the branches of the trees. We imagine Neil Armstrong, the early-morning sunlight in the branches of the trees. We imagine Neptune, the glowing morning sunlight in the branches of the trees. We imagine Nietzsche, the powdery morning sunlight in the branches of the trees. We imagine O. Ardiles, the deep morning sunlight in the branches of the trees. We imagine Odysseus, the unmoving morning sunlight in the branches of the trees. We imagine Oliver North, the starchy morning sunlight in the branches of the trees. We imagine Oliver Reed, the grey morning sunlight in the branches of the trees. We imagine Orlando Gibbons, the stiff morning sunlight in the branches of the trees. We imagine Orville and Wilbur Wright, the sullen morning sunlight in the branches of the trees. We imagine Palestrina, the september-morning sunlight in the branches of the trees. We imagine Paul Gascoigne, the northern morning sunlight in the branches of the trees. We imagine Pelé, the dwindling morning sunlight in the branches of the trees. We imagine Peter Arnett, the coming morning sunlight in the branches of the trees. We imagine Peter Fonda, the weekend-morning sunlight in the branches of the trees. We imagine Peter Sellers, the buttery morning sunlight in the branches of the trees. We imagine Peter Shilton, the fading morning sunlight in the branches of the trees. We imagine Phil Silvers, the lowering morning sunlight in the branches of the trees. We imagine Philo, the filthy morning sunlight in the branches of the trees. We imagine Piero della Francesca, the unfolding morning sunlight in the branches of the trees. We imagine Plato, the simple morning sunlight in the branches of the trees. We imagine Pluto, the gradual morning sunlight in the branches of the trees. We imagine Pola Negri, the unceasing morning sunlight in the branches of the trees. We imagine Pope Leo X, the flickering morning sunlight in the branches of the trees. We imagine Pu-Yi, the metallic morning sunlight in the branches of the trees. We imagine Pythagoras, the drifting morning sunlight in the branches of the trees. We imagine R.A. Watson-Watt, the close morning sunlight in the branches of the trees. We imagine R.F. Scott, the smoky morning sunlight in the branches of the trees. We imagine Raisa Gorbachev, the plain morning sunlight in the branches of the trees. We imagine Raleigh, the pure morning sunlight in the branches of the trees. We imagine Raphael, the softer morning sunlight in the branches of the trees.

'I don't know why you have to bring René Descartes into it; I mean, I don't know why you have to bring René Descartes into it.'
'I don't know why you have to bring Richelieu into it; I mean, I don't know why you have to bring Richelieu into it.'
'I don't know why you have to bring Rip Torn into it; I mean, I don't know why you have to bring Rip Torn into it.'
'I don't know why you have to bring Roald Amundsen into it; I mean, I don't know why you have to bring Roald Amundsen into it.'
'I don't know why you have to bring Robert E. Peary into it; I mean, I don't know why you have to bring Robert E. Peary into it.'
'I don't know why you have to bring Robert Maxwell into it; I mean, I don't know why you have to bring Robert Maxwell into it.'
'I don't know why you have to bring Robert Stephenson into it; I mean, I don't know why you have to bring Robert Stephenson into it.'
'I don't know why you have to bring Roger Moore into it; I mean, I don't know why you have to bring Roger Moore into it.'
'I don't know why you have to bring Rupert Murdoch into it; I mean, I don't know why you have to bring Rupert Murdoch into it.'
'I don't know why you have to bring St Aiden into it; I mean, I don't know why you have to bring St Aiden into it.'
'I don't know why you have to bring St Alban into it; I mean, I don't know why you have to bring St Alban into it.'
'I don't know why you have to bring St Anselm into it; I mean, I don't know why you have to bring St Anselm into it.'
'I don't know why you have to bring St Benedict into it; I mean, I don't know why you have to bring St Benedict into it.'
'I don't know why you have to bring St Boniface into it; I mean, I don't know why you have to bring St Boniface into it.'
'I don't know why you have to bring St Bruno into it; I mean, I don't know why you have to bring St Bruno into it.'
'I don't know why you have to bring St Cyr into it; I mean, I don't know why you have to bring St Cyr into it.'
'I don't know why you have to bring St Cyril into it; I mean, I don't know why you have to bring St Cyril into it.'
'I don't know why you have to bring St David into it; I mean, I don't know why you have to bring St David into it.'
'I don't know why you have to bring St Dionysius into it; I mean, I

don't know why you have to bring St Dionysius into it.'

'I don't know why you have to bring St Dominic into it; I mean, I don't know why you have to bring St Dominic into it.'

'I don't know why you have to bring St Dunstan into it; I mean, I don't know why you have to bring St Dunstan into it.'

'I don't know why you have to bring St Elias into it; I mean, I don't know why you have to bring St Elias into it.'

'I don't know why you have to bring St Francis into it; I mean, I don't know why you have to bring St Francis into it.'

'I don't know why you have to bring St George into it; I mean, I don't know why you have to bring St George into it.'

'I don't know why you have to bring St Gregory into it; I mean, I don't know why you have to bring St Gregory into it.'

'I don't know why you have to bring St Helena into it; I mean, I don't know why you have to bring St Helena into it.'

'I don't know why you have to bring St James into it; I mean, I don't know why you have to bring St James into it.'

'I don't know why you have to bring St Jerome into it; I mean, I don't know why you have to bring St Jerome into it.'

'I don't know why you have to bring St Joan into it; I mean, I don't know why you have to bring St Joan into it.'

'I don't know why you have to bring St John of the Cross into it; I mean, I don't know why you have to bring St John of the Cross into it.'

'I don't know why you have to bring St John of Damascus into it; I mean, I don't know why you have to bring St John of Damascus into it.'

'I don't know why you have to bring St John into it; I mean, I don't know why you have to bring St John into it.'

'I don't know why you have to bring St Kentigern into it; I mean, I don't know why you have to bring St Kentigern into it.'

'I don't know why you have to bring St Lawrence into it; I mean, I don't know why you have to bring St Lawrence into it.'

'I don't know why you have to bring St Mark into it; I mean, I don't know why you have to bring St Mark into it.'

'I don't know why you have to bring St Michael into it; I mean, I don't know why you have to bring St Michael into it.'

'I don't know why you have to bring St Neri into it; I mean, I don't know why you have to bring St Neri into it.'

'I don't know why you have to bring St Nicholas into it; I mean, I don't know why you have to bring St Nicholas into it.'

Evening at the lakeside, St Olga emerging from the darkening woods. Evening at the lakeside, St Oswald emerging from the brackeny woods. Evening at the lakeside, St Paul emerging from the dampening woods. Evening at the lakeside, St Peter emerging from the mushroomy woods. Evening at the lakeside, St Simon emerging from the leafless woods. Evening at the lakeside, St Thaddeus emerging from the fenced-off woods. Evening at the lakeside, St Ursula emerging from the distant woods. Evening at the lakeside, Saints Anthony and Augustine emerging from the silent woods. Evening at the lakeside, Samuel Sheidt emerging from the unmapped woods. Evening at the lakeside, Saturn emerging from the neighbouring woods. Evening at the lakeside, Scarlatti emerging from the hillside woods. Evening at the lakeside, Sean Connery emerging from the continuing woods. Evening at the lakeside, Seneca emerging from the sunlit woods.

Sherpa Tensing stands up from the piano, says something quiet, and walks outside. Sid James stands up from the hospital bed, says something quiet, and walks outside. Socrates stands up from the backgammon board, says something quiet, and walks outside. Spike Milligan stands up from the sofa, says something quiet, and walks outside. Spinoza stands up from the kitchen table, says something quiet, and walks outside. Stan Laurel and Oliver Hardy stand up from the picture book, say something quiet, and walk outside. Stanley Baxter stands up from the desk, says something quiet, and walks outside. Steve Martin stands up from the flowerbeds, says something quiet, and walks outside. Sully stands up from the tv, says something quiet, and walks outside. Sun Yat-sen stands up from the discussion, says something quiet, and walks outside. Su Xiaokang stands up from the meal, says something quiet, and walks outside. Tariq Aziz stands up from the daybed, says something quiet, and walks outside. Telemann stands up from the problem, says something quiet, and walks outside. Terry-Thomas stands up from the fireplace, says something quiet, and walks outside. Thomas Edison stands up from the puzzle, says something quiet, and walks outside. Thomas More stands up from the meeting, says something quiet, and walks outside. Thomas Tallis stands up from the Talmud, says something quiet, and walks outside. Thomas Telford stands up from the sink, says something quiet, and walks outside. Thor Heyerdahl stands up from the bench, says something quiet, and walks outside. Titian stands up from the magazine rack, says something quiet, and walks outside. Tommy Cooper stands up from the counter, says something quiet, and walks outside. Tony Curtis stands up from the lawn, says something quiet, and walks outside. Tony Hancock stands up from the stool, says something quiet, and walks outside. Torelli stands up from the wall, says something quiet, and walks outside.

Over coffee and spaghetti, Tz'e Hsi coming over kind of weary and intense. Over coffee and yogurt, Uccello coming over kind of weary and intense. Over coffee and potatoes, Uranus coming over kind of weary and intense. Over coffee and green apples, Van Eyck coming over kind of weary and intense. Over coffee and cigarettes, Vasari coming over kind of weary and intense. Over coffee and onions, Vasco da Gama coming over kind of weary and intense. Over coffee and halloumi, Venus coming over kind of weary and intense. Over coffee and good whisky, Vic Reeves coming over kind of weary and intense. Over coffee and doughnuts, Victor Emanuel III coming over kind of weary and intense. Over coffee and cold milk, Vivaldi coming over kind of weary and intense. Over coffee and hot fish, Vivien Leigh coming over kind of weary and intense. Over coffee and eggs, Wally Herbert coming over kind of weary and intense. Over coffee and warm armagnac, Walter Huston coming over kind of weary and intense. Over coffee and fresh cheese, Walter Matthau coming over kind of weary and intense. Over coffee and cream, Wang Juntao coming over kind of weary and intense. Over coffee and pastries, William Randolph Hearst coming over kind of weary and intense. Over coffee and sausages, Wittgenstein coming over kind of weary and intense. Over coffee and good olives, Woody Allen coming over kind of weary and intense. Over coffee and oranges, Wuer Kaxi coming over kind of weary and intense. Over coffee and black-currants, Yen Chia-kan coming over kind of weary and intense. Over coffee and nougat, Yuri Gagarin coming over kind of weary and intense. Over coffee and fried bread, Zeinab Badawi coming over kind of weary and intense. Over coffee and pancakes, Zeno of Elea coming over kind of weary and intense. Over coffee and hash browns, Zeppo coming over kind of weary and intense. Over coffee and mushroom risotto, Zhang Weiguo coming over kind of weary and intense. Over coffee and falafels, Zhao Zi-yang coming over kind of weary and intense. Over coffee and sandwiches, Zog I coming over kind of weary and intense. Over coffee and chocolate fudge, Zwingli coming over kind of weary and intense.

Acknowledgements

A number of the pieces collected here were written as contributions to projects undertaken with a number of collaborators.

'Virtual airport' and 'South Korea and Japan 2002' were written for collaborative projects with the painter Clare Bleakley.

'Four-letter words' forms the lyrics to a cycle of songs written with the composer Larry Goves for the Society for the Promotion of New Music, first performed by Psappha at the University of Manchester, March 2007. It has appeared in the *Manchester Review*.

'Home Economics' was written for and performed at *Settling In*, curated by Jo Lansley and Inés Rae, a fringe event for British Art Show 6, 2006.

The Jesus poem and 'Six poems by themselves' were completed during a fellowship at Hawthornden Castle in 2004. The Jesus poem received a commendation in the National Poetry Competition 2004. A version of the concrete poems was included by Richard Price in *Painted, Spoken* 15, 2007.

Three of these pieces were written for projects organised by Dominic Chennell: the 'Paul Simon variations' was exhibited in *Radio Radio*, curated by Mel Brimfield, at International 3, Manchester, 2003, and the Trade Department, London, 2004; 'Clued in' was written for the Helfa Gelf treasure hunt, Conwy, 2006; the 'Woven poems' were produced by Carphology as name tapes for the Real Institute's *Roadshow* event, Blaenau Ffestiniog, 2003. The Welsh versions are by Bedwyr Williams.

Salem Films used the toolbox poem in its education project work. This project came about following a poetry-and-film course at Tŷ Newydd, Gwynedd, in 2006, organised by Mark Reid of BFI Education, Ynyr Williams of Salem Films and Tom Barrance of Media Education Wales.

Larry Goves's setting of 'Poppy' was performed by The House of Bedlam in the Cutting Edge series at the Warehouse, London, and the Huddersfield Contemporary Music Festival, November 2008. The London performance was broadcast on 'Hear and Now', Radio 3, April 2009.

Chris Evans suggested Raymond Roussel's *Locus Solus* as a starting point for 'I must say that at first it was difficult work', and included the finished poem in his book *Magnetic Promenade and other sculpture parks* (Studio Voltaire, 2006).

'Measure' was published by James Davies as Matchbox 11.

The discussion on putting this book together involved a number of people. Thanks are due to John McAuliffe and Anthony Caleshu. And special thanks are due to Nicola Mostyn.

Note
'I must say that at first it was difficult work'

'I must say that at first it was difficult work' is a comment made by Raymond Roussel with regard to his method of prose composition. Specifically he is discussing his way of constructing a text by taking a word which occurs in one sentence, finding a word loosely homophonic to that word, and then building a subsequent sentence which in some way incorporates the new word. The new sentence, then, will include another word which will form the basis for the next sentence, and so on. And by continuing this principle of one-step-forward-one-step-back, an entire novel eventually comes to be written.

This method is described by Roussel in his book *How I Wrote Certain of my Books*, and the example he gives is from his novel *Impressions d'Afrique*, where a sentence deploying the word *billard* (billiard table) leads onto a sentence which uses the word *pillard* (plunderer). Or rather, this is how Roussel's description of this method of composition is given by Michel Foucault in his study *Death and the Labyrinth – the World of Raymond Roussel*. And, more specifically, it is how Foucault's version of Roussel's description of his method is conveyed in Charles Ruas's translation of Foucault's book. The point, of course, is that in deriving one sentence from another – or in arriving at an account which is a translation of a paraphrase of a description which itself may or may not be entirely accurate – the outcome might be less a distortion of the original than a text with an originality of its own. And maybe too it is significant that this method should feel more like a game of chinese whispers than a traditionally poetic use of rhyme.

So the phrase 'I must say that at first it was difficult work', which is both the title for my piece and the grounds on which it was written, comes not from Roussel, as such, but from Ruas's version of Foucault's version of Roussel. Even so, when I came across the phrase it seemed to have an attraction of its own, which may be why I departed a little from the method described. It was certainly a phrase fruitful enough to provide the basis for the thirty-six sentences I eventually derived from it. And whether or not writing this piece was in fact difficult work is a matter which probably shouldn't detain me here.